THIS BOOK BELONGS TO:

....

THE
FOUNTAIN
TAROT JOURNAL

THE
FOUNTAIN
TAROT JOURNAL
A YEAR IN *52* READINGS

JASON GRUHL   JONATHAN SAIZ   ANDI TODARO

Roost Books
Boulder
2018

Roost Books
An imprint of Shambhala Publications, Inc.
4720 Walnut Street
Boulder, Colorado 80301
roostbooks.com

9 8 7 6 5 4 3 2 1

First Edition
Printed in the United States of America

∞ This edition is printed on acid-free paper that meets the American
National Standards Institute Z39.48 Standard.
♲ Shambhala Publications makes every effort to print on recycled paper.
For more information please visit www.shambhala.com.

Roost Books is distributed worldwide by
Penguin Random House, Inc., and its subsidiaries.

Designed by Andi Todaro

Library of Congress Cataloging-in-Publication Data
Names: Gruhl, Jason, author.
Title: The fountain tarot journal: a year in 52 readings /
Jason Gruhl and Andi Todaro; photographs by Jonathan Saiz.
Description: First Edition. | Boulder: Roost Books, 2018.
Identifiers: LCCN 2017050942 | ISBN 9781611806359 (pbk.: alk. paper)
Subjects: LCSH: Tarot.
Classification: LCC BF1879.T2 G78 2018 | DDC 133.3/2424—dc23
LC record available at https://lccn.loc.gov/2017050942

YOU ARE THE
VOICE
AND THE
BREATH
OF UNIVERSES

—The Fountain Tarot

Dedicated to those brave enough to look inward . . .

NOTE FROM THE CREATORS

Humans have always attempted to manifest their highest spiritual selves through art, writing, music, and other means. We created *The Fountain Tarot Journal* to help you reveal all of what you are and to express and celebrate the unnameable force within you that is both intimate and universal. By diving deeply into questions, reflections, dreams, patterns, and unknowns, we can begin to uncover the hidden workings of our thoughts, desires, and emotions. It is with this awareness that we are able to more simply *be*, and to live fuller, richer lives.

Life is one long journey of discovery. As we gain an understanding of ourselves, a new depth of discovery emerges and we are off again, exploring and experiencing. Because of this, the gifts of openness and self-awareness are some of the greatest gifts we can cultivate.

The examples, language, and artwork in this journal are distilled from *The Fountain Tarot* deck, but you should feel free to use any deck that resonates with you as you move along your path. *The Fountain Tarot Journal* is compatible with *all* of Tarot, and the writings and visuals within are simply meant to enhance your experience.

Though your journey is intensely personal, you are not alone. You are part of a brave and fearless group committed to self-discovery, honesty, and reflection. We hope that in some small way this journal contributes to your path and to a profound sense of wisdom in your life.

ANDi   Jason   Isaic

Follow us on Instagram @fountaintarot

WHY A REGULAR
DAILY PRACTICE?

Many of us crave a more consistent balance between our busy, daily lives and what our hearts pull us toward. We long for a greater awareness of spirit and a deeper understanding of our true selves. Integrating a Tarot practice throughout the week in quick draws or expansive readings can create space for reflection, connection, and peace of mind. This journal provides space for fifty-two readings and is structured for one reading per week throughout the year, but feel free to do as many readings as you wish! Whether you are working at home, preparing for yoga, sitting at your office, or relaxing on vacation, the images and text allow you to focus your attention, open to new possibilities, and bring clarity to your decisions and daydreams.

Tarot guides the ongoing conversation of your life by highlighting what's working, illuminating the dark corners of what you may be missing or avoiding, and identifying patterns that don't serve you. While the real tools are the joyous, chaotic, and ordinary experiences of your life, Tarot is the mirror that reflects them, working *for* you and *with* you to shine brightly and reveal your true self.

HOW TO USE
THIS BOOK

Like most journals, *The Fountain Tarot Journal* is meant to be used in whatever way works best for you. However, we have included elements that will foster clarity and insight in your readings by helping you record and observe your process throughout the year. The next sections orient beginners and provide prompts and examples for expanding your practice. These sections are a great place to return to for inspiration throughout the year.

TAROT BASICS to help you navigate the symbols and meanings of the cards.

READING AND SAMPLE SPREADS to offer a variety of approaches and expand the depth of your journaling.

PROMPTS FOR CONNECTING, SUMMARIZING, AND REFLECTING to expand on the insights from your readings.

EXAMPLE READING AND INTERPRETATION to offer guidance on how to start your practice.

CARD OF THE YEAR EXERCISE to generate a focus for the year.

Each of the journal pages has the following ideas to explore and catalog your journey, though they can easily be tailored to your liking.

Question/Issue: This is the focus of your inquiry or the general topic that the reading will develop. Be open—sometimes the reading answers the question *behind* the question you are asking.

Traits and Meanings: These are the building blocks of your reading. Determining the qualities of each card in terms of meaning, suit, number, or court position adds depth and insight to your reading. Account for the traditional meanings, but use your intuition as well.

Initial Reaction: This is your "gut reaction" to the cards and the reading overall—your first thoughts and emotions upon seeing the cards individually and together. This is different from your personal reflection, and should be more about noticing what's coming up for you in the moment than about synthesizing the information.

Connections/Relationships between the Cards: Finding the connections between cards and relating their attributes begins to flesh out the potential relationships of traits and behaviors in your reading. Use these to connect traits and behaviors in your life as they relate to your question.

Patterns and Themes: Keeping track of, or acknowledging, the patterns and themes in our lives can sometimes be confusing or elusive. We've provided a space on each page for you to see what shows up throughout the year. This will help with your summaries and reflections as well. The categories include:

SELF: life/body

POSSESSIONS: wealth/value/money

COMMUNICATION: siblings/education/short journeys

HOME: family/parent

CREATIVITY: pleasure/children/romance/entertainment

HEALTH: service/work/routine

PARTNERSHIPS: marriage/spouse/known enemies

DEATH AND REGENERATION: sex/death/magic/inheritances/loss

MIND/SPIRIT EXPLORATION: philosophy/long journeys/higher ed./ spirituality/goals/law

CAREER: work/social status/dominant parent

FRIENDSHIP: wishes/associations/aspirations

THE UNCONSCIOUS: hidden matters/self-undoing/unseen beliefs/ secret enemies/seclusion/repressions

Summary (what the cards say/represent): After determining the traits and meanings and making connections between the cards, summarize your findings as they relate to your question. Write down things that are obvious and also hypotheses about what might be relevant or possible.

Personal Reflection: This is the synthesis of everything you've learned about the reading as it applies directly to your life and your question. How do the meanings and relationships in the reading describe your current situation and what views do they open up?

Action Steps: This is where the "rubber meets the road" in terms of your reading. Based on your personal reflection, what concrete steps can you take to move your insights into action? How can you move your intentions and breakthroughs into your everyday life?

People to Enlist: You are not alone, remember? We all have people that can support us in our lives. Identify the key people in your communities that can play a role in your journey. Be specific about what they might be able to contribute, and be open to them.

Through experience you will learn (or you may already know) what spreads work best for you. There are templates for 3-, 5-, and 10-card spreads for you to explore, followed by the journal pages that can be tailored to your liking. There are also quarterly summaries every thirteen readings that allow you to reflect on and observe what you have learned and plan for the future. Through developing and deepening a weekly practice, we hope that *The Fountain Tarot Journal* will assist you in creating and discovering a vibrant life filled with peace, fun, ease, and wisdom.

TAROT BASICS

THE CARDS

MAJOR ARCANA (THE FOOL'S JOURNEY)

The Major Arcana (trump cards) tells the story of a unique human path to enlightenment that each of us can discover, conveyed through the encounters of an innocent soul—The Fool. The Fool (0) meets twenty-one guides, each with a lesson and an action he must take. It is always significant when a seeker encounters a card from the Major Arcana in a reading, and it can be helpful to view the meaning of the card in relationship to the Fool's Journey. The twenty-one can be broken down into three groups of seven, each teaching a mastery in particular realms:

THE PHYSICAL: The Magician, The High Priestess, The Empress, The Emperor, The Hierophant, The Lovers, and The Chariot.

THE SPIRITUAL: Justice, The Hermit, Wheel of Fortune, Strength, The Hanged Man, Death, and Temperance

THE ETHEREAL: The Devil, The Tower, The Star, The Moon, The Sun, Judgment, and The World.

THE FOUNTAIN: ∞ represents reunion with and recognition as the divine.

MINOR ARCANA

While the cards of the Major Arcana speak to large themes and archetypal characters, the cards of the Minor Arcana represent the day-to-day experiences of life. They contain nuanced details specific to the varied, and sometimes complicated, situations in which we find ourselves, and they deepen our understanding of the trump cards. Though they lack the gravity of the trumps, they contribute vital information to the reading, filling out the conversation and revealing its breadth and reach. The Minor Arcana consists of four suits: Wands, Swords, Cups, and Coins. Each suit contains fourteen cards, including pips (Ace through Ten) and court cards (Page, Knight, Queen, King). These cards can represent moods, patterns, states of being, people, personality traits, or other attributes, all of which help the seeker to focus the reading.

PIPS AND COURT CARDS

In addition to its meaning, each group of pips and court cards corresponds with certain attributes or flavors. When reading and listening, consider these characteristics,* allowing their light to shine or dim depending on the other cards around them.

ACE—seed, potential, beginnings
TWO—instincts, weighing choices, duality
THREE—development, first steps, growth
FOUR—rootedness, stability, foundation
FIVE—instability, solving problems
SIX—a challenge, regaining control
SEVEN—persistence, individuality
EIGHT—will, intellect, beating obstacles
NINE—integration, a return to self
TEN—completion, a "turn of the wheel"
PAGE—a child, new stages, immaturity
KNIGHT—a teenager, movement, loyalty
QUEEN—growth, nurturing, realization
KING—motivation, leadership, passion

THE SUITS

The suits each correspond to a particular element, and like the pips and court cards, they each have certain characteristics associated with them. Their essence is the backdrop, and readings should be filtered through or at least acknowledge and entertain the energy of the suits present. Here are some of the most popular associations with the suits.

WANDS (FIRE)—passion and will, goals and intentions, action, masculine energy

SWORDS (AIR)—communication, mind, and thoughts, logic, analysis and planning

CUPS (WATER)—emotions, intuition and relationships, spirituality, feminine energy

COINS (EARTH)—health, body and physical experience, money, the senses, practicality

*Thirteen's Tarot Card Meanings by Thirteen, Aeclectic Tarot, 2011.

GETTING STARTED

READING AND
SAMPLE SPREADS

Reading Tarot is not meant to be difficult. It can be as simple as clearing a space, pulling out your deck, shuffling, and asking a question. However, it is important to build your intuition around the cards so you are both open and able to make meaningful interpretations. Each card's meanings can be literal, physical, existential, or global. If you are a beginner, bring play to your learning: choose cards randomly and say the first word that comes to mind, tell a story using the images, or ask seemingly mundane questions to explore the real essence of each card!

A "spread" is the format in which Tarot readings are given. Many variations exist based on what someone is asking and how much information they want, ranging from the simple to the deeply complex. We have included three in this journal.

3-CARD

This spread is perfect for simple questions or for general inquiries about larger topics and can provide an expanded view of the question across time, form, or relationship. It can also be used for multiple people when attempting to gain individual direction on a shared question. The following are popular examples of 3-card spreads:

SITUATIONAL
1. Past
2. Present
3. Future

PERSONAL
1. Mind
2. Body
3. Spirit

RELATIONAL
1. You
2. The Other Person
3. The Relationship

5-CARD

This spread begins to incorporate more elements and is perfect for answering more specific questions or beginning to flesh out the "world" of a particular situation. As in the 3-card spread, each card represents one facet, and one example of this spread is laid out here.

THE FOUNTAIN SPREAD

1. The Question: what's really being asked—clarifies the question and focuses the inquiry more specifically.

2. The Context: what led up to now—reveals what factors in your past played the most significant role in getting you where you are now

3. You: your role in the situation—highlights what personal qualities or actions are needed in the current situation

4. Your Community: who else plays a role—identifies who in your community is needed or will play a part in the current situation

5. The Potential Outcome: the culmination—announces the result or action needed to answer the question

10-CARD

This spread, also called the Celtic Cross, is one of the oldest and most popular spreads in Tarot. It touches on many elements and gives the seeker an in-depth and detailed look at their question, exploring influences across time, the environment, and one's internal state.

1. The Present Situation
2. The Challenge You Face
3. The Past
4. The Future
5. Goals and Aspirations: What You Want
6. Subconscious: Emotions and Patterns
7. Advice or Recommendation
8. Community and External Influences
9. Hopes and Fears
10. Outcome

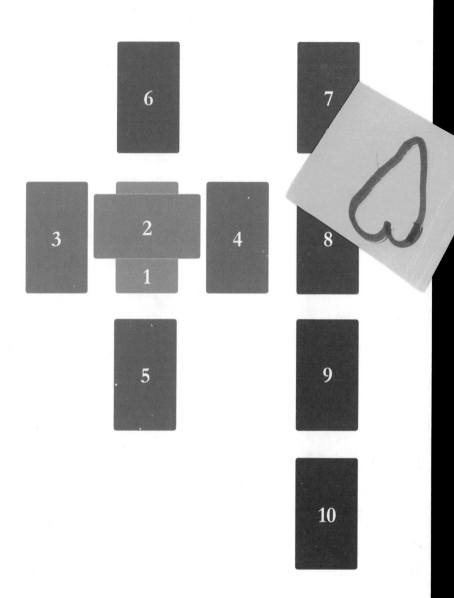

PROMPTS FOR CONNECTING, SUMMARIZING, AND REFLECTING

1. How can I foster creativity and inspiration in my life?
2. What does this particular relationship need right now?
3. Where should I focus my intention?
4. Where am I getting in my own way?
5. How can I best use my skills and talents to serve the world?
6. How do I invite deeper love into my life?
7. Both of my choices are great. How do I decide?
8. What's needed to turn my daydreams into reality?
9. How can I bring more passion to my work, relationship, etc.?
10. What kind of stories am I telling myself? Are they helpful?
11. What do I need to let go of?
12. Where am I losing momentum? How can I regain it?
13. How can I create better balance in my life?
14. How can I strengthen or support my goals?
15. Am I giving as much as I receive?
16. Is now a good time to start a new hobby?
17. What tools do I possess that I'm not utilizing?
18. What's the right amount of risk to be taking right now?
19. How do I incorporate more playfulness into my life?
20. What expectations from others can I leave behind?
21. If my life is a story, what adventure can I write into it?
22. How do I get rid of a habit that no longer serves me?
23. What does my dog/cat/pet need from me?
24. What's the meaning of life?

EXAMPLE READING AND INTERPRETATION

There's no right way to interpret a spread. Each card's theme, archetype, or message paired with your intuition guides the reading.

3-CARD SPREAD: "MIND, BODY, SPIRIT"

Question/Issue: How do I make creativity a priority in my life?

Traits and Meanings:

1. **Mind**	TWO OF WANDS	TWOS: duality WANDS: passion	"Two Choices," only enough energy to develop one well, boldness, instinct
2. **Body**	QUEEN OF COINS	QUEENS: realization COINS: practicality	"Generous Dedication," self-confidence, a unique way of being, resourcefulness
3. **Spirit**	THE STAR	THE ETHEREAL: archetypal, timeless	"All Is Well," everything in its own time, commitment to what's important, persistent focus

Initial Reaction: There's a warm and reassuring vibe about these cards. They feel inviting, powerful, and positive. The Queen feels protective and nurturing, a mother figure. The Star feels ominous but beautiful—a light in the darkness, perhaps?

Connections/Relationships between the Cards: There's a clear feminine energy present with the Queen and the Star. The fire of the Wands and the earth of the Coins seem to contrast. There's a Major Arcana card, which influences all the cards and represents something big and universal about what's being asked.

Patterns and Themes: This reading is focused on creativity and career. (Refer to page 11 to see the patterns and themes.)

Summary (what the cards say/represent): In this reading, there is a contrast between the action of Wands and the practicality of Coins. *Mentally,* my instincts can be trusted. I can be bold. I need to focus my energy and not let too many options confuse the situation. *Physically,* I am competent and have the experience I need to accomplish my goals. I can embrace my unique way of doing things, commit to a path, and access my resources! *Spiritually,* I need to remember that things take time. In the big picture, all is well. Staying persistent and focused will keep me open to guidance.

Personal Reflection: IS there enough time for my job AND my creativity? I worry that if I dive fully into creative projects that I'll lose balance and send my life into upheaval, lose momentum at work, or maybe even quit my job. *Mentally,* I really do know in my heart that it's possible to balance my creative pursuits with my day-to-day life, and I can trust that instinct and be bold about moving forward. *Physically,* I am a capable and responsible person. Practically speaking, I need to start taking action and staying persistent. I can commit to a plan, even a small one, knowing that I've got a supportive network of friends and family. *Spiritually,* everything is fine, but I'm feeling unfulfilled. I want more creativity in my life so I need to invite it in. I AM a star and I deserve to shine brightly and completely.

Action Steps:

1. Design a special space dedicated to art and creativity.
2. Set a daily, uninterrupted time before work to create.
3. Research communities that can support me in keeping this a regular practice and be resources for me.

People to Enlist:

1. My best friend—seems to have good balance with her own creative and work life.
2. My Aunt—has worked as an artist her whole life and I could ask her for tips.
3. My coworker—attends a regular drawing group—I could give it a try.

CARD OF THE
YEAR EXERCISE

This exercise allows you to generate a focus or intention for the year using a simple formula. Once you've identified your card of the year, write it below and set your main intention for the next fifty-two weeks. If you're unsure of your yearly intention, use the exercise on page 29 to clarify.

1. **Add the month of your birthday to the date of your birthday**
   ex. (4) April 30 = 4 + 30 = 34

2. **Add that number to the current year**
   ex. 34 + 2017 = 2051

3. **Add the numbers from the resulting number together**
   ex. 2 + 0 + 5 + 1 = 8

4. **Now find the card in the Major Arcana that correlates to that number.**
   ex. The 8th card in the Major Arcana is Justice. In this example, the Card of the Year would be Justice.

The Birth/Personality Card Exercise is another activity that illuminates a trait, quality, or value that plays a significant role in your life or with which you were born. It helps identify your strengths, gifts, and natural tendencies. To determine this card, simply replace the current year in step 2 with your birth year.

$$11 + 13 = 24$$
$$24 + 1973 = 1997$$

- Strengths
$$1 + 9 + 9 + 7 = 26 = 4$$

- gifts
$$2 + 6 = 8$$

- natural tendancies

rootedness
stability
Foundation

turning within this year is appropriate + deserved

Guide during difficult times

CARD OF THE YEAR:
HERMET (SAGE (Shaman))

Wise Elder
Wise Spirit Within
Lantern
Lamp of TRUTH
used to guide the unknown

$11+13=24$

$24+2019$

2043

$2+0+4+3=9$

"Socratic" method

Prudence — Careful / Cautious / discreet / Economical / Frugal

Treason
Dissimulation — disloyal / unreality
Corruption — dishonest
Roguery — mischief

STAFF
The patriarch's to help him navigate narrow paths as he seeks enlightenment

CLOAK
Form of descr- descretion

unconcealed
undisguised
no policy
Brave
hasty + rash

Solitude
Withdrawl
detatch
Patience
discretion
limitation

retreat from society look inward

Intention: I am at a cliff + use the Hermet + Staff of Wisdom + light to get direction. The Hermit is the Wise Spirit Within! Me! Find Her! (Re)define her! What is the Deepest part of me? The part that knows what to do in times of decision. I know what right way to respond World + Challenges I will hear voice of (31) conscious

Seek Mentor

The answers we seek can be found within

SPECIFIC INTENTIONS FOR THE YEAR

Self I will complete Transform:20
out of bed

Communication Build relationship w/ Joe
Complete 6-9 Montessori
Decide Brave Girl Certify or No.
Journey to OHI

Home Values book complete
Family: define safe + respectful → No spank
Parent agreements
Separate Alissa

Creativity Pleasure of Women's group
Kid's room's 100%
romance seeking
entertainment in sports - Team Pennents

Health Scans @ Mayo
OHI in Texas
Like minded parents / Clients only
routine self-care w/ early wake-ups

Family/Partnerships RCA Complete
Figure out what a fullfilling marriage looks like
Negotiables + non negotiables update
Mary intensive
Define relationship with Sue + Gen
Mind/Spirit
define my philosophy • Parenting
• Who is Alissa
long journey
Spirituality → What/where spiritual home
goals
Vocation • Build Business plan
• Tour Hillside
• Curriculum gather for Art BARN
• Morton Quote

Friendships ☆ reconnect Shauna, Tina, Chassy, Bridget
remember B-days w/ Astrology
☆ Santa Fe friendship nurture ☺
☆ associations - 505 OSTOMY
505 BOOK CLUB
505 Navigators
Other

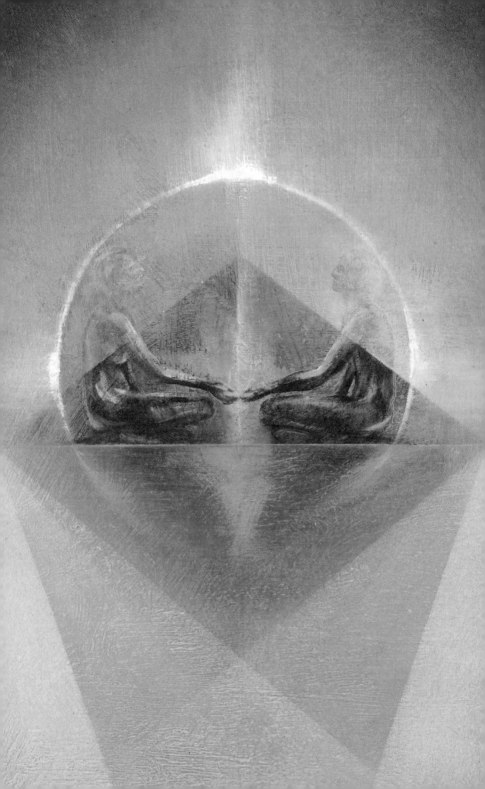

JOURNAL PAGES

3-CARD SPREAD JOURNAL ENTRY

Date __1-1-19__   Time __11:35 am__

Question/Issue __Relational__

What is our relationship's highest + best good.
What to focus on?

Will we heal

	ME	CHRIS	Relationship

Traits and Meanings

2 - weighing choices
   instincts
   hoodwinked
   conformity
   courage
   mind thoughts logic
   affection

Sword - Communication (Air)

8   will
    intellect
    beating obstacles
    dejected man
    desert the cups

Cups - emotions
       intuition
       relationships (Water)
       give joy, mildness, honor, modesty

Queen   realization
        growth
        nurture
        widowhood
        female sadness
        embarass - separate
        mourning
        destruction

Swords mind
        thought
        logic
        Communication (Air)

ME
1. **2 Swords**
   obstacles to clear passage
   choice
   difficult yot decision
   intentionally blind to avoid decision
   Fear of painful consequences

CHRIS
2. **8 Cups**
   change + transition
   sadness - solitude
   turned his back on all accomplished
   what fought for not worth it.
   what could bring more material satisfaction

Relationship
3. **Queen Swords**
   stearn + composed
   judge w/out sentiment
   calm - unbiased to make decision w/ facts
   clarity of thought
   Careful Consideration
   • intellect w/out compassion = Baren

Initial Reaction

I can't decide so he does + walks away leaving all his accomplishedents behind. Then I am left to rule alone but have to be responsible (single parent) rules + values of cherub + crafts of butterfly crown and silly of cloud cloak

Connections/Relationships between the Cards __2 swords__

having this relationship focus on thoughts, mental, logic and analysis - Mostly me. Chris is cups which is emotions relationship + 8 is logic.

Patterns and Themes ___partnerships___

Summary (what the cards say/represent) __That we are both weighing__
the options. He is realizing what he is fighting for may not
be what he wants anymore. I am gathering facts
to make careful consideration of kids + single mom
lifestyle.

Personal Reflection __I see that there is a possible ending__
in this marriage. It could spin to ending the un-happiness
and using new recovery to redefine, re-vow. Or,
he could leave by death or choice. In the relationship I am ruling as Queen + have faith's
Guidance (red bracelet) and child focused (throne)
crown of butterflies.

Action Steps • Plan of attack - Syllabus — RCA
— ChrisTina
   • Mediation
   • My survival benefits checked.

People to Enlist • AZ Attorney ~~gone~~
  • SF one who ~~went~~ before me   owgbm
   • owners - grants - SCORE
  •

**"YOUR TASK IS NOT TO SEEK FOR LOVE, BUT MERELY TO SEEK AND FIND
ALL THE BARRIERS WITHIN YOURSELF THAT YOU HAVE BUILT AGAINST IT."**

—RUMI

5-CARD SPREAD JOURNAL ENTRY

Date 1-1-18   Time 2:05pm

Question/Issue Career Path in 2019
Seeking clarity of direction needed.

Traits and Meanings

loss   a plan that cuts   material trouble
theft   chaos
abandon

                                       5. instability
                                          practicality solve problems
                                          health   practicality
                       growth   body   physical body
hope   teenager, movement   Physical
bright   loyalty   nurture   games

Prospects

1. The Question	2. The Context	3. You	4. Community	5. The Outcome
Etheral	Knight of	Queen of	7	5
Star	Pentacles	Pentacles	Swords	Pentacles
balance	Utility	generousity	persistence	adversity
harmony	serviceable	liberty	individuality	Financial strife
end of period of	Practicality	Practicality	communication	lack of confidence
turmoil	health	health	mind	
fulfill	Physical	Physical	thoughts	Manifest
Peace of mind	body	body	logic	prosperity fulfilled
mental +	WORK EFFORT	material SUCCESS	analysis	
emotional	diligence	Sensual pleasure	Sure of success	
Stability	Care	Fullfill of Creative project	deception	
Self confidence	dedicated	Finds of goal/dream	betrayal	
Self knowledge	loyal worker	to end goal	dont gain by	
	willing	boredom + struggle	dubious means	

remain calm + in peace b/c of wisdom

HP. → She gots me.

Initial Reaction   I will need to water both on Career $ + Children
= TEACH Montessori it will provide harmony + balance. My
willingness to settle or take one for the team has got me here. My
qualities + actions include caring for my body, continue to grow me - grow kids + nurture
dont involve community that's not up + up. Seeing financial strife will
be action needed to answer question

Connections/Relationships between the Cards

Pentacles = Coin = $ lots!! Practicality

Community - My limiting beliefs - deception, using SBA, etc.

realization = Queen = Me
Star - everything in its own time

38

Patterns and Themes Career: Work, Social Status
dominant parent

Summary (what the cards say/represent) Do the calm+peaceful route.
perserverence + effort are required if its of value – Patience
keep everything on up+up + trust that what got me
here was the desire to be calm spiritual, lifestyle

Personal Reflection I believe my own Montessori is
the way since 7 swords scares me, I see calm
for my mind + body is not a corporate job.
The one to help maybe the one who decreved.

_____

_____

_____

Action Steps _____

_____

_____

People to Enlist _____

_____

_____

"OUR ANXIETY DOES NOT COME FROM THINKING ABOUT
THE FUTURE, BUT FROM WANTING TO CONTROL IT."

—KAHLIL GIBRAN

10-CARD SPREAD JOURNAL ENTRY

*Date*_____ *Time*_____

*Question/Issue*_____

_____

_____

_____

Traits and Meanings

1. The Present	2. The Challenge	3. The Past	4. The Future	5. Goals

6. Subconscious	7. Advice	8. Community	9. Hopes & Fears	10. The Outcome

Initial Reaction _____

_____

_____

_____

Patterns and Themes _____

_____

Connections/Relationships between the Cards _____

_____

_____

_____

Summary (what the cards say/represent) _____

_____

_____

_____

_____

Personal Reflection _____

_____

_____

_____

_____

_____

Action Steps _____

_____

_____

People to Enlist _____

_____

*Date*_____ *Time*_____

*Question/Issue*_____

_____

_____

_____

*Traits and Meanings*_____

_____

_____

_____

_____

_____

_____

*Initial Reaction*_____

_____

_____

_____

*Connections/Relationships between the Cards*_____

_____

_____

_____

_____

_____

Patterns and Themes _____

Summary (what the cards say/represent) _____

_____

_____

_____

Personal Reflection _____

_____

_____

_____

_____

_____

_____

Action Steps _____

_____

_____

_____

People to Enlist _____

_____

_____

"THE MOST REGRETFUL PEOPLE ON EARTH ARE THOSE WHO FELT THE CALL
TO CREATIVE WORK, WHO FELT THEIR OWN CREATIVE POWER RESTIVE AND
UPRISING, AND GAVE IT NEITHER POWER NOR TIME."

—MARY OLIVER

Date_____ Time_____

Question/Issue_____

_____

_____

_____

Traits and Meanings_____

_____

_____

_____

_____

_____

_____

Initial Reaction_____

_____

_____

_____

Connections/Relationships between the Cards_____

_____

_____

_____

_____

_____

Patterns and Themes _____

Summary (what the cards say/represent) _____

_____

_____

_____

Personal Reflection _____

_____

_____

_____

_____

_____

_____

Action Steps _____

_____

_____

_____

People to Enlist _____

_____

_____

"THE PRECISE ROLE OF THE ARTIST, THEN, IS TO ILLUMINATE THAT DARKNESS, BLAZE ROADS
THROUGH VAST FORESTS, SO THAT WE WILL NOT, IN ALL OUR DOING, LOSE SIGHT OF ITS
PURPOSE, WHICH IS, AFTER ALL, TO MAKE THE WORLD A MORE HUMAN DWELLING PLACE."

—JAMES BALDWIN

Date_____ Time_____

Question/Issue_____

_____

_____

_____

Traits and Meanings_____

_____

_____

_____

_____

_____

Initial Reaction_____

_____

_____

_____

Connections/Relationships between the Cards_____

_____

_____

_____

_____

_____

Patterns and Themes _____

Summary (what the cards say/represent) _____

_____

_____

_____

Personal Reflection _____

_____

_____

_____

_____

_____

_____

Action Steps _____

_____

_____

_____

People to Enlist _____

_____

_____

**"IF WE LEARN TO OPEN OUR HEARTS, ANYONE, INCLUDING THE
PEOPLE WHO DRIVE US CRAZY, CAN BE OUR TEACHER."**

—PEMA CHÖDRÖN

*Date*_____ *Time*_____

*Question/Issue*_____

_____

_____

_____

*Traits and Meanings*_____

_____

_____

_____

_____

_____

_____

*Initial Reaction*_____

_____

_____

_____

*Connections/Relationships between the Cards*_____

_____

_____

_____

_____

_____

Patterns and Themes _____

Summary (what the cards say/represent) _____

_____

_____

_____

Personal Reflection _____

_____

_____

_____

_____

_____

_____

Action Steps _____

_____

_____

_____

People to Enlist _____

_____

_____

"OUR OWN LIFE HAS TO BE OUR MESSAGE."

—THICH NHAT HANH

Date _____ *Time* _____

Question/Issue _____

_____

_____

_____

Traits and Meanings _____

_____

_____

_____

_____

_____

_____

Initial Reaction _____

_____

_____

_____

Connections/Relationships between the Cards _____

_____

_____

_____

_____

_____

Patterns and Themes _____

Summary (what the cards say/represent) _____

_____

_____

_____

Personal Reflection _____

_____

_____

_____

_____

_____

_____

Action Steps _____

_____

_____

_____

People to Enlist _____

_____

_____

**"NO PERSON IS YOUR FRIEND WHO DEMANDS YOUR
SILENCE, OR DENIES YOUR RIGHT TO GROW."**

—ALICE WALKER

*Date*_____ *Time*_____

*Question/Issue*_____

_____

_____

_____

_____

*Traits and Meanings*_____

_____

_____

_____

_____

_____

_____

*Initial Reaction*_____

_____

_____

_____

*Connections/Relationships between the Cards*_____

_____

_____

_____

_____

_____

Patterns and Themes _____

Summary (what the cards say/represent) _____

_____

_____

_____

_____

Personal Reflection _____

_____

_____

_____

_____

_____

_____

Action Steps _____

_____

_____

_____

People to Enlist _____

_____

_____

"THE CHALLENGE IS NOT TO BE PERFECT ... IT'S TO BE WHOLE."

—JANE FONDA

Date_____ Time_____

Question/Issue_____
_____
_____
_____
_____

Traits and Meanings_____
_____
_____
_____
_____
_____
_____

Initial Reaction_____
_____
_____
_____

Connections/Relationships between the Cards_____
_____
_____
_____
_____
_____

Patterns and Themes _____

Summary (what the cards say/represent) _____

_____

_____

_____

Personal Reflection _____

_____

_____

_____

_____

_____

_____

Action Steps _____

_____

_____

_____

People to Enlist _____

_____

_____

"KNOWING WHAT MUST BE DONE DOES AWAY WITH FEAR."

—ROSA PARKS

*Date*_____ *Time*_____

*Question/Issue*_____
_____
_____
_____

*Traits and Meanings*_____
_____
_____
_____
_____
_____
_____

*Initial Reaction*_____
_____
_____
_____

*Connections/Relationships between the Cards*_____
_____
_____
_____
_____
_____

Patterns and Themes _____

Summary (what the cards say/represent) _____

_____

_____

_____

Personal Reflection _____

_____

_____

_____

_____

_____

_____

Action Steps _____

_____

_____

_____

People to Enlist _____

_____

_____

"LIFE WILL GIVE YOU WHATEVER EXPERIENCE IS MOST HELPFUL FOR THE EVOLUTION
OF YOUR CONSCIOUSNESS. HOW DO YOU KNOW THIS IS THE EXPERIENCE YOU NEED?
BECAUSE THIS IS THE EXPERIENCE YOU ARE HAVING AT THIS MOMENT."

—ECKHART TOLLE

Date_____ Time_____

Question/Issue_____

_____

_____

_____

Traits and Meanings_____

_____

_____

_____

_____

_____

_____

Initial Reaction_____

_____

_____

_____

Connections/Relationships between the Cards_____

_____

_____

_____

_____

_____

Patterns and Themes _____

Summary (what the cards say/represent) _____

_____

_____

_____

Personal Reflection _____

_____

_____

_____

_____

_____

_____

Action Steps _____

_____

_____

_____

People to Enlist _____

_____

_____

"IT'S ONE OF THE GREATEST GIFTS YOU CAN GIVE
YOURSELF, TO FORGIVE. FORGIVE EVERYBODY."

—MAYA ANGELOU

Date_____ Time_____

Question/Issue_____

_____

_____

_____

Traits and Meanings_____

_____

_____

_____

_____

_____

Initial Reaction_____

_____

_____

_____

Connections/Relationships between the Cards_____

_____

_____

_____

_____

_____

Patterns and Themes _____

Summary (what the cards say/represent) _____

_____

_____

_____

Personal Reflection _____

_____

_____

_____

_____

_____

_____

Action Steps _____

_____

_____

_____

People to Enlist _____

_____

_____

"BE SOFT. DO NOT LET THE WORLD MAKE YOU HARD. DO NOT LET PAIN MAKE YOU HATE.
DO NOT LET BITTERNESS STEAL YOUR SWEETNESS. TAKE PRIDE THAT EVEN THOUGH THE
REST OF THE WORLD MAY DISAGREE, YOU STILL BELIEVE IT TO BE A BEAUTIFUL PLACE."

—KURT VONNEGUT

QUARTERLY SUMMARY AND REFLECTION

*Themes and Patterns*_____

_____

_____

_____

*Relationship to Your Card of the Year*_____

_____

_____

_____

*Breakthroughs*_____

_____

_____

_____

*Personal Reflection*_____

_____

_____

_____

*Future Intention*_____

_____

_____

_____

_____

CARD OF THE QUARTER:

_____

_Intention_____

_____

_____

_____

_____

_____

_____

_____

*Date*_____ *Time*_____

*Question/Issue*_____

_____

_____

_____

*Traits and Meanings*_____

_____

_____

_____

_____

_____

_____

*Initial Reaction*_____

_____

_____

_____

*Connections/Relationships between the Cards*_____

_____

_____

_____

_____

_____

Patterns and Themes _____

Summary (what the cards say/represent) _____

_____

_____

_____

Personal Reflection _____

_____

_____

_____

_____

_____

_____

Action Steps _____

_____

_____

_____

People to Enlist _____

_____

_____

"NORMAL IS NOT SOMETHING TO ASPIRE TO,
IT'S SOMETHING TO GET AWAY FROM."

—JODIE FOSTER

Date_____ Time_____

Question/Issue_____

_____

_____

_____

Traits and Meanings_____

_____

_____

_____

_____

_____

_____

Initial Reaction_____

_____

_____

_____

Connections/Relationships between the Cards_____

_____

_____

_____

_____

_____

Patterns and Themes _____

Summary (what the cards say/represent) _____

_____

_____

_____

Personal Reflection _____

_____

_____

_____

_____

_____

_____

Action Steps _____

_____

_____

_____

People to Enlist _____

_____

_____

"AT THE CENTER OF YOUR BEING YOU HAVE THE ANSWER; YOU
KNOW WHO YOU ARE AND YOU KNOW WHAT YOU WANT."

—LAO TZU

*Date*_____ *Time*_____

*Question/Issue*_____

_____

_____

_____

*Traits and Meanings*_____

_____

_____

_____

_____

_____

*Initial Reaction*_____

_____

_____

_____

*Connections/Relationships between the Cards*_____

_____

_____

_____

_____

_____

Patterns and Themes _____

Summary (what the cards say/represent) _____

_____

_____

_____

Personal Reflection _____

_____

_____

_____

_____

_____

_____

Action Steps _____

_____

_____

_____

People to Enlist _____

_____

_____

"AUTHENTICITY IS A COLLECTION OF CHOICES THAT WE HAVE TO MAKE
EVERY DAY. IT'S ABOUT THE CHOICE TO SHOW UP AND BE REAL. THE
CHOICE TO BE HONEST. THE CHOICE TO LET OUR TRUE SELVES BE SEEN."

—BRENÉ BROWN

Date＿＿＿＿＿＿＿＿＿＿＿＿ *Time*＿＿＿＿＿＿＿＿＿＿＿

Question/Issue＿＿＿＿＿＿＿＿＿＿＿＿＿＿＿＿＿＿＿＿

＿＿＿＿＿＿＿＿＿＿＿＿＿＿＿＿＿＿＿＿＿＿＿＿＿＿

＿＿＿＿＿＿＿＿＿＿＿＿＿＿＿＿＿＿＿＿＿＿＿＿＿＿

＿＿＿＿＿＿＿＿＿＿＿＿＿＿＿＿＿＿＿＿＿＿＿＿＿＿

Traits and Meanings＿＿＿＿＿＿＿＿＿＿＿＿＿＿＿＿＿＿

＿＿＿＿＿＿＿＿＿＿＿＿＿＿＿＿＿＿＿＿＿＿＿＿＿＿

＿＿＿＿＿＿＿＿＿＿＿＿＿＿＿＿＿＿＿＿＿＿＿＿＿＿

＿＿＿＿＿＿＿＿＿＿＿＿＿＿＿＿＿＿＿＿＿＿＿＿＿＿

＿＿＿＿＿＿＿＿＿＿＿＿＿＿＿＿＿＿＿＿＿＿＿＿＿＿

＿＿＿＿＿＿＿＿＿＿＿＿＿＿＿＿＿＿＿＿＿＿＿＿＿＿

Initial Reaction＿＿＿＿＿＿＿＿＿＿＿＿＿＿＿＿＿＿＿

＿＿＿＿＿＿＿＿＿＿＿＿＿＿＿＿＿＿＿＿＿＿＿＿＿＿

＿＿＿＿＿＿＿＿＿＿＿＿＿＿＿＿＿＿＿＿＿＿＿＿＿＿

＿＿＿＿＿＿＿＿＿＿＿＿＿＿＿＿＿＿＿＿＿＿＿＿＿＿

Connections/Relationships between the Cards＿＿＿＿＿＿＿

＿＿＿＿＿＿＿＿＿＿＿＿＿＿＿＿＿＿＿＿＿＿＿＿＿＿

＿＿＿＿＿＿＿＿＿＿＿＿＿＿＿＿＿＿＿＿＿＿＿＿＿＿

＿＿＿＿＿＿＿＿＿＿＿＿＿＿＿＿＿＿＿＿＿＿＿＿＿＿

＿＿＿＿＿＿＿＿＿＿＿＿＿＿＿＿＿＿＿＿＿＿＿＿＿＿

Patterns and Themes _____

Summary (what the cards say/represent) _____

_____

_____

_____

Personal Reflection _____

_____

_____

_____

_____

_____

_____

Action Steps _____

_____

_____

_____

People to Enlist _____

_____

_____

**"WE DO NOT NEED MAGIC TO CHANGE THE WORLD, WE
CARRY ALL THE POWER WE NEED INSIDE OURSELVES
ALREADY; WE HAVE THE POWER TO IMAGINE BETTER."**

—J. K. ROWLING

Date _____ Time _____

Question/Issue _____

_____

_____

_____

Traits and Meanings _____

_____

_____

_____

_____

_____

Initial Reaction _____

_____

_____

_____

Connections/Relationships between the Cards _____

_____

_____

_____

_____

_____

Patterns and Themes _____

Summary (what the cards say/represent) _____

_____

_____

_____

Personal Reflection _____

_____

_____

_____

_____

_____

_____

Action Steps _____

_____

_____

_____

People to Enlist _____

_____

_____

"DON'T BE SATISFIED WITH STORIES, HOW THINGS HAVE
GONE WITH OTHERS. UNFOLD YOUR OWN MYTH."

—RUMI

*Date*_____ *Time*_____

*Question/Issue*_____
_____
_____
_____

*Traits and Meanings*_____
_____
_____
_____
_____
_____
_____

*Initial Reaction*_____
_____
_____
_____

*Connections/Relationships between the Cards*_____
_____
_____
_____
_____
_____

Patterns and Themes _____

Summary (what the cards say/represent) _____

_____

_____

_____

Personal Reflection _____

_____

_____

_____

_____

_____

_____

Action Steps _____

_____

_____

_____

People to Enlist _____

_____

_____

"BECAUSE YOU ARE ALIVE, EVERYTHING IS POSSIBLE."

—THICH NHAT HANH

Date _____ Time _____

Question/Issue _____
_____
_____
_____

Traits and Meanings _____
_____
_____
_____
_____
_____
_____

Initial Reaction _____
_____
_____
_____

Connections/Relationships between the Cards _____
_____
_____
_____
_____
_____

Patterns and Themes _____

Summary (what the cards say/represent) _____

_____

_____

_____

Personal Reflection _____

_____

_____

_____

_____

_____

_____

Action Steps _____

_____

_____

_____

People to Enlist _____

_____

_____

"IT TAKES COURAGE . . . TO ENDURE THE SHARP PAINS OF
SELF-DISCOVERY RATHER THAN CHOOSE TO TAKE THE DULL PAIN OF
UNCONSCIOUSNESS THAT WOULD LAST THE REST OF OUR LIVES."

—MARIANNE WILLIAMSON

Date_____ Time_____

Question/Issue_____
_____
_____
_____

Traits and Meanings_____
_____
_____
_____
_____
_____

Initial Reaction_____
_____
_____
_____

Connections/Relationships between the Cards_____
_____
_____
_____
_____
_____

Patterns and Themes _____

Summary (what the cards say/represent) _____

_____

_____

_____

Personal Reflection _____

_____

_____

_____

_____

_____

_____

Action Steps _____

_____

_____

_____

People to Enlist _____

_____

_____

"YOUR VISIONS WILL BECOME CLEAR ONLY WHEN YOU CAN LOOK INTO YOUR OWN HEART. WHO LOOKS OUTSIDE, DREAMS; WHO LOOKS INSIDE, AWAKES."

—CARL JUNG

Date _____ *Time* _____

Question/Issue _____

_____

_____

_____

Traits and Meanings _____

_____

_____

_____

_____

_____

Initial Reaction _____

_____

_____

_____

Connections/Relationships between the Cards _____

_____

_____

_____

_____

_____

Patterns and Themes _____

Summary (what the cards say/represent) _____

_____

_____

_____

Personal Reflection _____

_____

_____

_____

_____

_____

_____

Action Steps _____

_____

_____

_____

People to Enlist _____

_____

_____

"LEARN FROM THE MISTAKES OF OTHERS. YOU CAN'T
LIVE LONG ENOUGH TO MAKE THEM ALL YOURSELF."

—ELEANOR ROOSEVELT

*Date*_____ *Time*_____

*Question/Issue*_____

_____

_____

_____

*Traits and Meanings*_____

_____

_____

_____

_____

_____

_____

*Initial Reaction*_____

_____

_____

_____

*Connections/Relationships between the Cards*_____

_____

_____

_____

_____

_____

Patterns and Themes _____

Summary (what the cards say/represent) _____

_____

_____

_____

Personal Reflection _____

_____

_____

_____

_____

_____

_____

Action Steps _____

_____

_____

_____

People to Enlist _____

_____

_____

**"WHATEVER IS BRINGING YOU DOWN, GET RID OF IT. BECAUSE YOU'LL
FIND THAT WHEN YOU'RE FREE . . . YOUR TRUE SELF COMES OUT."**

—TINA TURNER

Date_____ Time_____

Question/Issue_____

_____

_____

_____

Traits and Meanings_____

_____

_____

_____

_____

_____

Initial Reaction_____

_____

_____

_____

Connections/Relationships between the Cards_____

_____

_____

_____

_____

_____

Patterns and Themes _____

Summary (what the cards say/represent) _____

_____

_____

_____

_____

Personal Reflection _____

_____

_____

_____

_____

_____

_____

Action Steps _____

_____

_____

_____

People to Enlist _____

_____

_____

"YOUR LIFE IS RIGHT NOW! IT'S NOT LATER! IT'S NOT IN THAT TIME OF RETIREMENT. IT'S NOT WHEN THE LOVER GETS HERE. IT'S NOT WHEN YOU'VE MOVED INTO THE NEW HOUSE. IT'S NOT WHEN YOU GET THE BETTER JOB. YOUR LIFE IS RIGHT NOW. IT WILL ALWAYS BE RIGHT NOW."

—ABRAHAM HICKS

*Date*_____ *Time*_____

*Question/Issue*_____

_____

_____

_____

*Traits and Meanings*_____

_____

_____

_____

_____

_____

*Initial Reaction*_____

_____

_____

_____

*Connections/Relationships between the Cards*_____

_____

_____

_____

_____

_____

Patterns and Themes _____

Summary (what the cards say/represent) _____

_____

_____

_____

_____

Personal Reflection _____

_____

_____

_____

_____

_____

_____

_____

Action Steps _____

_____

_____

_____

People to Enlist _____

_____

_____

**"AND THE DAY CAME WHEN THE RISK TO REMAIN TIGHT IN A BUD
WAS MORE PAINFUL THAN THE RISK IT TOOK TO BLOSSOM."**

—ANAÏS NIN

Date_____ Time_____

Question/Issue_____

_____

_____

_____

Traits and Meanings_____

_____

_____

_____

_____

_____

Initial Reaction_____

_____

_____

_____

Connections/Relationships between the Cards_____

_____

_____

_____

_____

_____

Patterns and Themes _____

Summary (what the cards say/represent) _____

_____

_____

_____

Personal Reflection _____

_____

_____

_____

_____

_____

_____

Action Steps _____

_____

_____

_____

People to Enlist _____

_____

_____

"I WILL NOT HAVE MY LIFE NARROWED DOWN. I WILL NOT BOW DOWN
TO SOMEBODY ELSE'S WHIM OR TO SOMEONE ELSE'S IGNORANCE."

—BELL HOOKS

QUARTERLY SUMMARY AND REFLECTION

*Themes and Patterns*_____

_____

_____

_____

*Relationship to Your Card of the Year*_____

_____

_____

_____

*Breakthroughs*_____

_____

_____

_____

*Personal Reflection*_____

_____

_____

_____

*Future Intention*_____

_____

_____

_____

_____

CARD OF THE QUARTER:

_____

_Intention_____

_____

_____

_____

_____

_____

_____

_____

*Date*_____ *Time*_____

*Question/Issue*_____

_____

_____

_____

*Traits and Meanings*_____

_____

_____

_____

_____

_____

_____

*Initial Reaction*_____

_____

_____

_____

*Connections/Relationships between the Cards*_____

_____

_____

_____

_____

_____

Patterns and Themes _____

Summary (what the cards say/represent) _____

_____

_____

_____

Personal Reflection _____

_____

_____

_____

_____

_____

_____

Action Steps _____

_____

_____

_____

People to Enlist _____

_____

_____

"STEP OUT OF THE HISTORY THAT IS HOLDING YOU BACK.
STEP INTO THE NEW STORY YOU ARE WILLING TO CREATE."

—OPRAH WINFREY

*Date*_____ *Time*_____

*Question/Issue*_____

_____

_____

_____

*Traits and Meanings*_____

_____

_____

_____

_____

_____

_____

*Initial Reaction*_____

_____

_____

_____

*Connections/Relationships between the Cards*_____

_____

_____

_____

_____

_____

Patterns and Themes _____

Summary (what the cards say/represent) _____

_____

_____

_____

Personal Reflection _____

_____

_____

_____

_____

_____

_____

Action Steps _____

_____

_____

_____

People to Enlist _____

_____

_____

"OUT OF SUFFERING HAVE EMERGED THE STRONGEST SOULS;
THE MOST MASSIVE CHARACTERS ARE SEARED WITH SCARS."

—KAHLIL GIBRAN

Date_____ Time_____

Question/Issue_____

_____

_____

_____

Traits and Meanings_____

_____

_____

_____

_____

_____

_____

Initial Reaction_____

_____

_____

_____

Connections/Relationships between the Cards_____

_____

_____

_____

_____

_____

Patterns and Themes _____

Summary (what the cards say/represent) _____

_____

_____

_____

_____

Personal Reflection _____

_____

_____

_____

_____

_____

_____

Action Steps _____

_____

_____

_____

People to Enlist _____

_____

_____

"SMALL ACTS, WHEN MULTIPLIED BY MILLIONS
OF PEOPLE, CAN TRANSFORM THE WORLD."

—HOWARD ZINN

*Date*_____ *Time*_____

*Question/Issue*_____

_____

_____

_____

*Traits and Meanings*_____

_____

_____

_____

_____

_____

*Initial Reaction*_____

_____

_____

_____

*Connections/Relationships between the Cards*_____

_____

_____

_____

_____

_____

Patterns and Themes _____

Summary (what the cards say/represent) _____

_____

_____

_____

Personal Reflection _____

_____

_____

_____

_____

_____

_____

Action Steps _____

_____

_____

_____

People to Enlist _____

_____

_____

"TAKE CRITICISM SERIOUSLY, BUT NOT PERSONALLY.
IF THERE IS TRUTH OR MERIT IN THE CRITICISM, TRY TO
LEARN FROM IT. OTHERWISE, LET IT ROLL RIGHT OFF YOU."

—HILLARY CLINTON

Date_____ Time_____

Question/Issue_____

_____

_____

_____

Traits and Meanings_____

_____

_____

_____

_____

_____

Initial Reaction_____

_____

_____

Connections/Relationships between the Cards_____

_____

_____

_____

_____

Patterns and Themes _____

Summary (what the cards say/represent) _____

_____

_____

_____

Personal Reflection _____

_____

_____

_____

_____

_____

Action Steps _____

_____

_____

_____

People to Enlist _____

_____

_____

**"IF YOU DON'T UNDERSTAND YOURSELF YOU
DON'T UNDERSTAND ANYBODY ELSE."**

—NIKKI GIOVANNI

Date_____ Time_____

Question/Issue_____

_____

_____

_____

_____

Traits and Meanings_____

_____

_____

_____

_____

_____

_____

Initial Reaction_____

_____

_____

_____

Connections/Relationships between the Cards_____

_____

_____

_____

_____

_____

Patterns and Themes _____

Summary (what the cards say/represent) _____

_____

_____

_____

Personal Reflection _____

_____

_____

_____

_____

_____

Action Steps _____

_____

_____

_____

People to Enlist _____

_____

_____

"THIS IS THE REAL SECRET OF LIFE—TO BE COMPLETELY
ENGAGED WITH WHAT YOU ARE DOING IN THE HERE AND NOW.
AND INSTEAD OF CALLING IT WORK, REALIZE IT IS PLAY."

—ALAN WATTS

Date_____ Time_____

Question/Issue_____

_____

_____

_____

_____

Traits and Meanings_____

_____

_____

_____

_____

_____

_____

Initial Reaction_____

_____

_____

_____

Connections/Relationships between the Cards_____

_____

_____

_____

_____

_____

Patterns and Themes _____

Summary (what the cards say/represent) _____

_____

_____

_____

Personal Reflection _____

_____

_____

_____

_____

_____

_____

Action Steps _____

_____

_____

_____

People to Enlist _____

_____

_____

"I KNOW THAT I AM INTELLIGENT, BECAUSE
I KNOW THAT I KNOW NOTHING."

—SOCRATES

*Date*_____ *Time*_____

*Question/Issue*_____

_____

_____

_____

_____

*Traits and Meanings*_____

_____

_____

_____

_____

_____

_____

*Initial Reaction*_____

_____

_____

_____

*Connections/Relationships between the Cards*_____

_____

_____

_____

_____

_____

Patterns and Themes _____

Summary (what the cards say/represent) _____

_____

_____

_____

Personal Reflection _____

_____

_____

_____

_____

_____

Action Steps _____

_____

_____

_____

People to Enlist _____

_____

_____

**"TO LIVE IS THE RAREST THING IN THE
WORLD. MOST PEOPLE JUST EXIST."**

—OSCAR WILDE

*Date*_____ *Time*_____

*Question/Issue*_____

_____

_____

_____

*Traits and Meanings*_____

_____

_____

_____

_____

_____

*Initial Reaction*_____

_____

_____

_____

*Connections/Relationships between the Cards*_____

_____

_____

_____

_____

Patterns and Themes _____

Summary (what the cards say/represent) _____

_____

_____

_____

Personal Reflection _____

_____

_____

_____

_____

_____

_____

Action Steps _____

_____

_____

_____

People to Enlist _____

_____

_____

**"WHAT YOU DO MAKES A DIFFERENCE, AND YOU HAVE TO
DECIDE WHAT KIND OF DIFFERENCE YOU WANT TO MAKE."**

—JANE GOODALL

*Date*_____ *Time*_____

*Question/Issue*_____

_____

_____

_____

*Traits and Meanings*_____

_____

_____

_____

_____

_____

_____

*Initial Reaction*_____

_____

_____

_____

*Connections/Relationships between the Cards*_____

_____

_____

_____

_____

_____

Patterns and Themes _____

Summary (what the cards say/represent) _____

_____

_____

_____

Personal Reflection _____

_____

_____

_____

_____

_____

_____

Action Steps _____

_____

_____

_____

People to Enlist _____

_____

_____

"THERE ARE A THOUSAND WAYS TO KNEEL AND KISS THE
GROUND; THERE ARE A THOUSAND WAYS TO GO HOME AGAIN."

—RUMI

*Date*_____ *Time*_____

*Question/Issue*_____

_____

_____

_____

*Traits and Meanings*_____

_____

_____

_____

_____

_____

_____

*Initial Reaction*_____

_____

_____

_____

*Connections/Relationships between the Cards*_____

_____

_____

_____

_____

_____

Patterns and Themes _____

Summary (what the cards say/represent) _____

_____

_____

_____

Personal Reflection _____

_____

_____

_____

_____

_____

Action Steps _____

_____

_____

_____

People to Enlist _____

_____

_____

"THE QUESTION ISN'T WHO IS GOING TO LET
ME; IT'S WHO IS GOING TO STOP ME."

—AYN RAND

Date _____ Time _____

Question/Issue _____

_____

_____

_____

Traits and Meanings _____

_____

_____

_____

_____

_____

Initial Reaction _____

_____

_____

_____

Connections/Relationships between the Cards _____

_____

_____

_____

_____

Patterns and Themes _____

Summary (what the cards say/represent) _____

_____

_____

_____

Personal Reflection _____

_____

_____

_____

_____

_____

_____

Action Steps _____

_____

_____

_____

People to Enlist _____

_____

_____

"AUTHENTICITY REQUIRES A CERTAIN MEASURE OF
VULNERABILITY, TRANSPARENCY, AND INTEGRITY."

—JANET LOUISE STEPHENSON

*Date*_____ *Time*_____

*Question/Issue*_____

_____

_____

_____

*Traits and Meanings*_____

_____

_____

_____

_____

_____

_____

*Initial Reaction*_____

_____

_____

_____

*Connections/Relationships between the Cards*_____

_____

_____

_____

_____

_____

Patterns and Themes _____

Summary (what the cards say/represent) _____

_____

_____

_____

Personal Reflection _____

_____

_____

_____

_____

_____

_____

Action Steps _____

_____

_____

_____

People to Enlist _____

_____

_____

"JUST AS A MOTHER WOULD PROTECT HER ONLY CHILD WITH HER LIFE,
EVEN SO LET ONE CULTIVATE A BOUNDLESS LOVE TOWARDS ALL BEINGS."

—BUDDHA

QUARTERLY SUMMARY AND REFLECTION

*Themes and Patterns*_____

_____

_____

_____

*Relationship to Your Card of the Year*_____

_____

_____

_____

*Breakthroughs*_____

_____

_____

_____

*Personal Reflection*_____

_____

_____

_____

*Future Intention*_____

_____

_____

_____

_____

CARD OF THE QUARTER:

Intention

Date_____ Time_____

Question/Issue_____

_____

_____

_____

Traits and Meanings_____

_____

_____

_____

_____

_____

Initial Reaction_____

_____

_____

_____

Connections/Relationships between the Cards_____

_____

_____

_____

_____

_____

Patterns and Themes _____

Summary (what the cards say/represent) _____

_____

_____

_____

Personal Reflection _____

_____

_____

_____

_____

_____

_____

Action Steps _____

_____

_____

_____

People to Enlist _____

_____

_____

"ALL GREAT TRUTHS BEGIN AS BLASPHEMIES."

—GEORGE BERNARD SHAW

Date_____ Time_____

Question/Issue_____

_____

_____

_____

Traits and Meanings_____

_____

_____

_____

_____

_____

_____

Initial Reaction_____

_____

_____

_____

Connections/Relationships between the Cards_____

_____

_____

_____

_____

_____

Patterns and Themes _____

Summary (what the cards say/represent) _____

_____

_____

_____

Personal Reflection _____

_____

_____

_____

_____

_____

_____

Action Steps _____

_____

_____

_____

People to Enlist _____

_____

_____

"SPREAD LOVE EVERYWHERE YOU GO. LET NO ONE
EVER COME TO YOU WITHOUT LEAVING HAPPIER."

—MOTHER TERESA

Date_____ Time_____

Question/Issue_____

_____

_____

_____

Traits and Meanings_____

_____

_____

_____

_____

_____

_____

Initial Reaction_____

_____

_____

_____

Connections/Relationships between the Cards_____

_____

_____

_____

_____

_____

Patterns and Themes _____

Summary (what the cards say/represent) _____

_____

_____

_____

_____

Personal Reflection _____

_____

_____

_____

_____

_____

_____

Action Steps _____

_____

_____

_____

People to Enlist _____

_____

_____

"I HAVE BEEN AND STILL AM A SEEKER, BUT I HAVE CEASED
TO QUESTION STARS AND BOOKS; I HAVE BEGUN TO LISTEN
TO THE TEACHING MY BLOOD WHISPERS TO ME."

—HERMANN HESSE

Date _____ Time _____

Question/Issue _____

_____

_____

_____

Traits and Meanings _____

_____

_____

_____

_____

_____

_____

Initial Reaction _____

_____

_____

_____

Connections/Relationships between the Cards _____

_____

_____

_____

_____

_____

Patterns and Themes _____

Summary (what the cards say/represent) _____

_____

_____

_____

Personal Reflection _____

_____

_____

_____

_____

_____

_____

Action Steps _____

_____

_____

_____

People to Enlist _____

_____

_____

"THE MOST FUNDAMENTAL AGGRESSION TO OURSELVES, THE MOST FUNDAMENTAL
HARM WE CAN DO TO OURSELVES, IS TO REMAIN IGNORANT BY NOT HAVING THE
COURAGE AND THE RESPECT TO LOOK AT OURSELVES HONESTLY AND GENTLY."

—PEMA CHÖDRÖN

Date _____ *Time* _____

Question/Issue _____

_____

_____

_____

Traits and Meanings _____

_____

_____

_____

_____

_____

_____

Initial Reaction _____

_____

_____

_____

Connections/Relationships between the Cards _____

_____

_____

_____

_____

_____

Patterns and Themes _____

Summary (what the cards say/represent) _____

_____

_____

_____

Personal Reflection _____

_____

_____

_____

_____

_____

_____

Action Steps _____

_____

_____

_____

People to Enlist _____

_____

_____

"YOU CAN'T BE THAT KID STANDING AT THE TOP OF THE WATERSLIDE,
OVERTHINKING IT. YOU HAVE TO GO DOWN THE CHUTE."

—TINA FEY

Date_____ Time_____

Question/Issue_____

_____

_____

_____

Traits and Meanings_____

_____

_____

_____

_____

_____

_____

Initial Reaction_____

_____

_____

_____

Connections/Relationships between the Cards_____

_____

_____

_____

_____

_____

Patterns and Themes ⎯⎯⎯⎯⎯⎯⎯⎯⎯⎯⎯⎯⎯⎯⎯⎯

Summary (what the cards say/represent) ⎯⎯⎯⎯⎯⎯⎯⎯⎯⎯

⎯⎯⎯⎯⎯⎯⎯⎯⎯⎯⎯⎯⎯⎯⎯⎯⎯⎯⎯⎯⎯⎯⎯⎯⎯⎯⎯⎯⎯⎯⎯

⎯⎯⎯⎯⎯⎯⎯⎯⎯⎯⎯⎯⎯⎯⎯⎯⎯⎯⎯⎯⎯⎯⎯⎯⎯⎯⎯⎯⎯⎯⎯

⎯⎯⎯⎯⎯⎯⎯⎯⎯⎯⎯⎯⎯⎯⎯⎯⎯⎯⎯⎯⎯⎯⎯⎯⎯⎯⎯⎯⎯⎯⎯

Personal Reflection ⎯⎯⎯⎯⎯⎯⎯⎯⎯⎯⎯⎯⎯⎯⎯⎯⎯⎯

⎯⎯⎯⎯⎯⎯⎯⎯⎯⎯⎯⎯⎯⎯⎯⎯⎯⎯⎯⎯⎯⎯⎯⎯⎯⎯⎯⎯⎯⎯⎯

⎯⎯⎯⎯⎯⎯⎯⎯⎯⎯⎯⎯⎯⎯⎯⎯⎯⎯⎯⎯⎯⎯⎯⎯⎯⎯⎯⎯⎯⎯⎯

⎯⎯⎯⎯⎯⎯⎯⎯⎯⎯⎯⎯⎯⎯⎯⎯⎯⎯⎯⎯⎯⎯⎯⎯⎯⎯⎯⎯⎯⎯⎯

⎯⎯⎯⎯⎯⎯⎯⎯⎯⎯⎯⎯⎯⎯⎯⎯⎯⎯⎯⎯⎯⎯⎯⎯⎯⎯⎯⎯⎯⎯⎯

⎯⎯⎯⎯⎯⎯⎯⎯⎯⎯⎯⎯⎯⎯⎯⎯⎯⎯⎯⎯⎯⎯⎯⎯⎯⎯⎯⎯⎯⎯⎯

Action Steps ⎯⎯⎯⎯⎯⎯⎯⎯⎯⎯⎯⎯⎯⎯⎯⎯⎯⎯⎯⎯⎯⎯⎯

⎯⎯⎯⎯⎯⎯⎯⎯⎯⎯⎯⎯⎯⎯⎯⎯⎯⎯⎯⎯⎯⎯⎯⎯⎯⎯⎯⎯⎯⎯⎯

⎯⎯⎯⎯⎯⎯⎯⎯⎯⎯⎯⎯⎯⎯⎯⎯⎯⎯⎯⎯⎯⎯⎯⎯⎯⎯⎯⎯⎯⎯⎯

⎯⎯⎯⎯⎯⎯⎯⎯⎯⎯⎯⎯⎯⎯⎯⎯⎯⎯⎯⎯⎯⎯⎯⎯⎯⎯⎯⎯⎯⎯⎯

People to Enlist ⎯⎯⎯⎯⎯⎯⎯⎯⎯⎯⎯⎯⎯⎯⎯⎯⎯⎯⎯⎯

⎯⎯⎯⎯⎯⎯⎯⎯⎯⎯⎯⎯⎯⎯⎯⎯⎯⎯⎯⎯⎯⎯⎯⎯⎯⎯⎯⎯⎯⎯⎯

⎯⎯⎯⎯⎯⎯⎯⎯⎯⎯⎯⎯⎯⎯⎯⎯⎯⎯⎯⎯⎯⎯⎯⎯⎯⎯⎯⎯⎯⎯⎯

**"WE CAN CHOOSE TO BE PERFECT AND
ADMIRED OR TO BE REAL AND LOVED."**

—GLENNON DOYLE MELTON

Date_____ Time_____

Question/Issue_____

_____

_____

_____

Traits and Meanings_____

_____

_____

_____

_____

_____

_____

Initial Reaction_____

_____

_____

_____

Connections/Relationships between the Cards_____

_____

_____

_____

_____

_____

Patterns and Themes _____

Summary (what the cards say/represent) _____

_____

_____

_____

Personal Reflection _____

_____

_____

_____

_____

_____

_____

Action Steps _____

_____

_____

_____

People to Enlist _____

_____

_____

"IT TOOK ME QUITE A LONG TIME TO DEVELOP A VOICE,
AND NOW THAT I HAVE IT, I AM NOT GOING TO BE SILENT."

—MADELEINE ALBRIGHT

Date_____ Time_____

Question/Issue_____
_____
_____
_____

Traits and Meanings_____
_____
_____
_____
_____
_____
_____

Initial Reaction_____
_____
_____

Connections/Relationships between the Cards_____
_____
_____
_____
_____

Patterns and Themes _____

Summary (what the cards say/represent) _____

_____

_____

_____

Personal Reflection _____

_____

_____

_____

_____

_____

_____

Action Steps _____

_____

_____

_____

People to Enlist _____

_____

_____

"THE BAD NEWS IS YOU'RE FALLING THROUGH THE AIR, NOTHING TO
HANG ON TO, NO PARACHUTE. THE GOOD NEWS IS THERE'S NO GROUND."

—CHÖGYAM TRUNGPA RINPOCHE

*Date*_____*Time*_____

*Question/Issue*_____

_____

_____

_____

_____

*Traits and Meanings*_____

_____

_____

_____

_____

_____

_____

*Initial Reaction*_____

_____

_____

_____

*Connections/Relationships between the Cards*_____

_____

_____

_____

_____

_____

Patterns and Themes _____

Summary (what the cards say/represent) _____

_____

_____

_____

_____

Personal Reflection _____

_____

_____

_____

_____

_____

_____

_____

Action Steps _____

_____

_____

_____

People to Enlist _____

_____

_____

"PURITY AND IMPURITY DEPEND ON ONESELF;
NO ONE CAN PURIFY ANOTHER."

—BUDDHA

Date_____ Time_____

Question/Issue_____

_____

_____

_____

Traits and Meanings_____

_____

_____

_____

_____

_____

_____

Initial Reaction_____

_____

_____

_____

Connections/Relationships between the Cards_____

_____

_____

_____

_____

_____

Patterns and Themes _____

Summary (what the cards say/represent) _____

_____

_____

_____

Personal Reflection _____

_____

_____

_____

_____

_____

_____

Action Steps _____

_____

_____

_____

People to Enlist _____

_____

_____

"FIND OUT WHO YOU ARE AND DO IT ON PURPOSE."

—DOLLY PARTON

Date_____ Time_____

Question/Issue_____

_____

_____

_____

_____

Traits and Meanings_____

_____

_____

_____

_____

_____

_____

Initial Reaction_____

_____

_____

_____

Connections/Relationships between the Cards_____

_____

_____

_____

_____

_____

Patterns and Themes _____

Summary (what the cards say/represent) _____

_____

_____

_____

Personal Reflection _____

_____

_____

_____

_____

_____

_____

Action Steps _____

_____

_____

_____

People to Enlist _____

_____

_____

"WE ARE ALL LIVING IN CAGES WITH THE DOOR WIDE OPEN."

—GEORGE LUCAS

*Date*_____ *Time*_____

*Question/Issue*_____

_____

_____

_____

_____

*Traits and Meanings*_____

_____

_____

_____

_____

_____

_____

*Initial Reaction*_____

_____

_____

_____

*Connections/Relationships between the Cards*_____

_____

_____

_____

_____

_____

Patterns and Themes _____

Summary (what the cards say/represent) _____

_____

_____

_____

Personal Reflection _____

_____

_____

_____

_____

_____

_____

Action Steps _____

_____

_____

_____

People to Enlist _____

_____

_____

**"IN THE DEPTHS OF WINTER, I FINALLY LEARNED THAT
WITHIN ME THERE LAY AN INVINCIBLE SUMMER."**

—ALBERT CAMUS

Date_____ Time_____

Question/Issue_____
_____
_____
_____

Traits and Meanings_____
_____
_____
_____
_____
_____
_____

Initial Reaction_____
_____
_____
_____

Connections/Relationships between the Cards_____
_____
_____
_____
_____
_____

Patterns and Themes _____

Summary (what the cards say/represent) _____

_____

_____

_____

Personal Reflection _____

_____

_____

_____

_____

_____

_____

Action Steps _____

_____

_____

_____

People to Enlist _____

_____

_____

"ALL DOUBT, DESPAIR, AND FEAR BECOME INSIGNIFICANT
ONCE THE INTENTION OF LIFE BECOMES LOVE."

—RUMI

QUARTERLY SUMMARY AND REFLECTION

*Themes and Patterns*_____

_____

_____

_____

*Relationship to Your Card of the Year*_____

_____

_____

_____

*Breakthroughs*_____

_____

_____

_____

*Personal Reflection*_____

_____

_____

_____

*Future Intention*_____

_____

_____

_____

_____

CARD OF THE QUARTER:

Intention

YEAR-END SUMMARY AND REFLECTION

Self _____

_____

_____

_____

Communication _____

_____

_____

_____

Home _____

_____

_____

_____

Creativity _____

_____

_____

_____

Health _____

_____

_____

_____

Family/Partnerships _____

_____

_____

_____

Mind/Spirit _____

_____

_____

_____

Vocation _____

_____

_____

_____

Friendships _____

_____

_____

_____

Other _____

_____

_____

_____

THE
FOUNTAIN
TAROT

THE FOUNTAIN TAROT DECK

The Fountain Tarot contributes newly to the sacred and exciting tradition of Tarot by respectfully reenvisioning the deck while bringing extensive quality to every detail. Ultimately, *The Fountain Tarot* offers a unique contemporary experience connecting the worlds of geometry, internet culture, art, and spirituality. Self-published in 2013 through a successful Kickstarter. Second publishing by Roost Books, 2017.

ABOUT THE CREATORS

For more information about the creators, go to www.fountaintarot.com.

Jonathan Saiz | *Artist*
www.jonathansaiz.com

Jason Gruhl | *Author*
www.jasongruhl.com

Andi Todaro | *Designer*
www.anditodaro.com